GOODNOUGH

RICHARD H. LOVE

HAASE-MUMM PUBLISHING CO., INC.

CHICAGO

Published by the Haase-Mumm Publishing Company, Inc., Chicago
Distributed by the Amart Book and Catalog
Distributing Company, Inc.
100 East Ohio Street, Room B-20, Chicago, IL 60611
Printed in the United States of America
First Edition

ISBN 0-940114-27-5

Design: Julie Love and Bruce C. Bachman
Photography: Bruce C. Bachman and T.K. Rose
Research and Editorial Preparation: Vytautas Babusis
Typesetting, Layout, and Printing: Fleetwood Litho & Letter Corp., New York

Robert Goodnough at work in his studio.

Traditionally, in contemplating non-objective art, a person thinks of something conceived by an artist from an inner aesthetic source, something, an image perhaps, perceivable but unrelated to the material world save the medium by which it is manifested. Therefore, as the artist departs the physical realm, he or she enters a new-old infinite zone of aesthetics limited only by his or her ability to produce images derived therefrom. Most contemporaries live each day, oblivious to this incredible aesthetic zone until amazingly few bits of it are manifested successfully by an artist—then we become privy to a secret but wonderful world which sensitizes us to higher spiritual plateaus.

Of course, each image should be new and unique and can be for as long as an artist continues making them, but the formal concept and discipline of creating non-representational art began early in the twentieth century. Contemporary American artists like Robert Goodnough, whose non-objective art has inspired viewers for several decades, learned a good deal from the European pioneer Wassily Kandinsky's writings *On the Spiritual in Art*.[1] In this famous 1912 publication Kandinsky tried to convince his readers that a truly sensitive individual could transcend the material to the spiritual through acute aesthetic percipience: "Literature, music, and art are the first and most sensitive realms where this spiritual change becomes noticeable in real form. These spheres immediately reflect the murky present; they provide an intimation of that greatness which first becomes noticeable only to a few, as just a tiny point, and which for the masses does not exist at all."[2] Kandinsky's words were published prior to World War I, several years before Robert Goodnough was born.

Although Kandinsky's ideas were not well known before the New York Armory Show of 1913, this exceedingly controversial exhibition provided the American art community with an unprecedented look at abstraction and served as a kind of spearhead for the advent of non-objective art or, to put it into the modern vernacular, of non-representational imagery. Thus, as non-objective art became an influential movement in Europe, it gradually gathered converts in New York until Hitler's rise to power forced many of Europe's most progressive artists and intellectuals to cross the Atlantic. Here their ideas were planted in stony but rich new soil where there was also an abundance of husbandry to maintain the sturdy new shoots of non-objective abstraction until this bumper crop was ready for harvest some years later. It was a very different harvest from the rows of representational art cultivated by Grant Wood and his band of regionalists in the Midwest and promoted in New York by those who opposed abstraction.

Though not a Jew, one progressive European whose art and ideas about it were more welcome in New York than in Berlin was Hilla Rebay, another great champion of non-objective painting. An outstanding painter herself, Rebay was exposed to Kandinsky's ideas as early as 1916 when her friend Hans Arp introduced her to the group at Herwarth Walden's art gallery Der Sturm and sent her copies of *Der Blaue Reiter* and *Über das Geistige in der Kunst* (*On the Spiritual in Art*).[3] By the late 1920s, when Rebay began organizing the Guggenheim Modern Art Collection, she was the foremost promoter of non-representational art in New York. Moreover, like Kandinsky, she sought more than the pictorial rudiments of abstraction, stressing its spiritual

L-4, 1986-87 acrylic and oil on canvas: 50 × 90 inches

implications.

America's Depression was waning slightly, and Robert Goodnough was enrolled at Syracuse University on a half-tuition scholarship when Hilla Rebay's catalog for a Guggenheim exhibition of non-objective paintings appeared. In this publication she urged viewers to see that "there is no representation of objects, nor any meaning of subjects in these paintings of free invention called non-objective art." She went on to state that "they represent a unique world of their own, as creations with a lawful organization of colors, variation of forms, and rhythm of motif. These combinations when invented by a genius can bring the same joy, relaxation, elevation and animation of spiritual life as music...Painting like music, has nothing to do with reproduction of nature, nor interpretation of intellectual meanings. Whoever is able to feel the beauty of colors and forms has understood non-objective paintings."[4]

Exhibitions and writings like Rebay's provided lessons which proselytized a large portion of the contemporary art community, especially the younger progressive members who sought innovation rather than tradition in their art. One of these was Goodnough, whose future years of productivity would result in a wide variety of experiments which would eventually evolve into a rich pictorial vocabulary of non-objective art.[5] As the years rolled by, Goodnough became inextricably involved with the movement of abstract art in America. The list of group exhibitions in which he participated is impressive, to say the least, and his solo shows received high praise from even the most reluctant critics. Moreover, his understanding of abstract art became well known to others as he contributed numer-

ous articles to *Art News* and other art publications. In summary, Goodnough became a highly regarded contributor to modern art from the 1950s to the 1980s, the period in which non-objective art made its most indelible imprint on American culture.

Years before the term "Post-Modernism" was invented, the great critic Clement Greenberg said that Robert Goodnough "has become one of the handful on whom the fate of painting as a high art seems to depend."[6] Perhaps even more than other critics, over the years Greenberg recognized an evolutionary process in Goodnough's work, which convinced him that the artist was far more than a significant contributor to American art; he was one of the few whose abstract images provided the underpinnings of contemporary painting. In the same way that Hilla Rebay's support helped earlier abstractionists, Greenberg's enthusiasm contributed to Goodnough's reputation. Also, other influential critics came to recognize his rare talent. Although he had a solo show as early as 1950 at George Wittenborn's bookstore, by 1962 *Newsweek* magazine announced to the world that "Goodnough has arrived." And in retrospect we see that Greenberg's prophesy was correct, for a quarter of a century later Goodnough stands as one of the stellar contributors to the history of American abstraction.

To put Goodnough's career in perspective, it is instructive to consider his oeuvre briefly. During World War II, Goodnough spent time in the Army where he served with combat forces in the South Pacific and even painted murals and portraits of officers. Later he moved to New York City and, using funds from the GI Bill, enrolled in the Ozenfant School of Fine Arts. A French painter and theorist, Amédée Ozenfant first laid down the principles of *Purism* in 1915-1917 in his magazine *L'Elan.* Often the elemental prescripts of organization by which the Purist procedure functions have been likened to those employed in the fugue by J.S. Bach. Moreover, Ozenfant referred to music in his art and chose titular references like *Chord* or *Fugue.* While Goodnough was studying under Ozenfant in New York, the French master strove to refine his theory of *Preforms* in which he attempted to prove that, like all truth, important art statements exist potentially in mankind's subliminal reservoir before being manifested by an "inventor," the artist. Later Goodnough incorporated various ideas and principles put forth by Ozenfant into his own art.

In 1947 Goodnough and a couple of friends spent the summer with the great teacher Hans Hofmann in Provincetown, Cape Cod. Here Goodnough was introduced to abstraction of a different vein, indeed by one whose brilliant abstract expressionist statements came to influence a whole generation of ardent followers. Anxious to better himself intellectually, Goodnough enrolled at New York University, but his interest in art was indelible, so outside of school he became a so-called member of "The Club," an enthusiastic assemblage including artists like Willem de Kooning, Adolph Gottlieb, Barnett Newman, Ad Reinhardt, Mark Rothko, and various others who were devoted to the promotion of abstract art in America. Goodnough was one of those rare individuals capable of balancing formal discipline in education with an active painting career: in 1949 he enrolled in the New School for Social Research, and in the following year he, Franz Kline,

Larry Rivers, and a few others were selected by Clement Greenberg and Meyer Schapiro for a show entitled "New Talent" at the Sam Kootz Gallery in New York, which served as one of America's great forums for non-objective art. Demonstrating amazing versatility, Goodnough also became an instructor at New York University and an editorial associate of *Art News* magazine, writing about the work of other artists. By 1952 Goodnough received his first major show at Tibor de Nagy Gallery, and a year later he became a teacher at Fieldstone School in Riverdale, New York.

In the 1950s Goodnough experimented with animal and figurative subjects, but these were conceived of in abstract terms. Writing for *Art News,* the critic Frank O'Hara reported a certain eccentric quality in Goodnough's paintings. Goodnough related only peripherally to nature, but the unrestricted freedom, the wild force, and the instinctive drive associated with individual animal forms truly inspired the artist. He had also become fascinated with the massive power and compelling forms of dinosaurs when he saw the skeleton of a brontosaurus at the New York Museum of Natural History. To convey his innermost feelings about these great extinct beasts, he conceived of them not as an illustrator who might recreate their bodies in an illusionistic primeval landscape, but in abstract imagery. To make his pictures, he glued various strips of paper to his surface area, working and reworking the composition until it evolved into the kind of bestial form he thought best represented the imagined spirit of his subject. In this way Goodnough brought the beast from its skeletal beginnings to a finished picture. Less significant experiments included collage sculptures in metal and cardboard and various figurative designs in mixed media sculpture. These experiments seemed to affect his large exhibition canvas, recalling certain aspects of cubism but executed with heavy brushstrokes yielding a non-cubistic impasto surface.

Although he was fast approaching a style of his own, Goodnough experimented freely. At times he flirted with the worn out but indelible influences of Cubism and at other times certain hints of Abstract Expressionism crept into his pictures. That he was searching was evident to those who admired his work but were not always certain of his intentions as Lawrence Campbell implied when in a 1955 issue of *Art News* he prophesied that "fantasy could lead him [Goodnough] in almost any direction."[7] And whatever others saw in his pictures Goodnough confirmed his own need to find himself in the work of others when he stated years later: "I wanted to experience all of the different ways other artists had dealt with problems of painting. I felt that out of the experience would come my own style. Kind of a process of growth. First you have to learn from other people."

With his work evolving step by step in the 1950s, Goodnough's ideas about non-objective art gravitated away from Hofmann's credos and closer to his own via Ozenfant. He simply could not subscribe to the avant-garde abstract expressionist mode, then so popular as promoted by the critic Harold Rosenberg and others. Instead, he worked out non-representational images whose content consisted solely of a wide array of distinctly individualistic abstract planes, color areas, and lines on open grounds. The juxtaposed tension generated from these striking shapes and spaces on two-dimensional surfaces served as the genesis of his abstraction. Various critics and interested observers analyzed his progress. One of these was the great scholar of modernism, Irving Sandler, who wrote: "Following the examples of de Kooning and, to a lesser degree, Pollock, Goodnough took as his points of departure the painterly, open scaffolds of Analytic Cubism and the light composition of the cleanly edged flat forms of the Synthetic phase which he loosened and opened up." Sandler went on to say that "Goodnough appeared to believe, as Greenberg later remarked, that the great achievement of the first generation was the 'grafting of painterliness on a Cubist infra-structure.' His aim was to further that achievement."[8]

As Goodnough continued, he shared the concerns of other progressives both of his generation and older adherents who balked at the pure subjectivism of the gestural Abstractionists, action painters like Hofmann, Pollock, and others, the governing impulse of whose art was "not a formal dialectic but Existential anxiety."[9] In most of Goodnough's work, even in its early stages, the sense of movement persists, sometimes subtle, at other times powerful and charged with internal energy, with the presence of form usually fractioned and dynamic, but always arranged in a way which imbued the image with kinetic potential. Considering paintings executed beyond the late 1950s, there is no point in comparing or contrasting his work or motivation with the action painters, Rosenberg's Intrasubjectives whose nearly mystical content Stuart Davis defined as a "Belch from the Unconscious."[10] Goodnough strove for something quite different from that which Hofmann or his friend Jackson Pollock presented; Goodnough's combination of color, forms, lines and spatial relationships was

ULYSSES L, 1961-62 acrylic and oil on canvas: 78 × 78 inches

GRAY YELLOW, 1977 acrylic and oil on canvas: 60 × 60 inches

intended not as a mystical manifestation of the sub-liminal depths of the artist but his perception of inertia, a pictorial equation of movement and energy derived from the fabric of the real world without imitating its combinations of forms. Of course it is possible that this aesthetic dimension is perceived by other artists, but when manifested by Goodnough it becomes a compelling visual entity. Unlike the abstract expressionists, whose raison d'etre was to reveal in their art the personal substance of the creative act, Goodnough clung to an underlying aesthetic structure allied to and often derived from the stimulus of his own creative impetus, from sources in nature and even from precedent compositions from the old masters, Rubens, for example, whose subjects he thought "created great force and energy."

Goodnough's abstract forms ranged from spontaneously distorted patterns of color to Mondrianesque rectangles and outlines to full-blown abstract planes interacting with lines and spaces. And as he endeavored to resolve the intangible into imagery, he purposefully maintained a kind of relative pictorial dichotomy. For example, in certain works we perceive inherent dynamism, tension, and an explosive vibrant force, while in others we are met with an ordered formality, a gentle translatory motion of nearly equal shapes yielding a pictorial harmony which approaches a syn-aesthetic equation with music. All of it comes from Goodnough's unequalled ability to make pictures of kinetic potential, to juxtapose shapes, planes, color, space and line, at times boldly and spontaneously, with seemingly little order, at other times carefully and poetically, even systematically. We get a better insight into

his work from Martin Bush who states that "Goodnough's paintings are projections of his inner feelings about a subject rather than a recreation of how the subject might actually appear."[11]

Through the 1960s there were many experiments resulting in failures and successes. Goodnough demonstrated impressive control of color as he orchestrated abstract compositions inspired by historical and traditional subjects and themes. A painting which reflects this pictorial transliteration is a canvas in this exhibition, entitled *Ulysses L.* Like the classical personality after whom it was named, the picture shows agitated movement, inner power, and a nervous energy. In this work Goodnough demonstrates greater emotional content; he resorts to elongated crescent-shaped blades of color which crisscross the entire canvas. This manner produces a moving organic mass which sways, vibrates, and pulsates as it swells with kinetic inertia to break free from the outer boundary of the canvas. Here the artist unites ordinary brushstrokes, color and form in an ambiguous two-dimensional space to present an intriguing image which in its titular reference harks back to the imaginative abstract dimensions of Ulysses's own adventures. In this regard we are reminded of Fairfield Porter's observation voiced in reviewing Goodnough's art: "long, curved vertical strokes detached from each other are set against gray, as in *Odysseus*." Porter continued that when Goodnough's pictures were given "classical names the composition is derived from an analysis of a classical sculpture; or else the flow of red, white, blue and gray paper scraps in curve and counter-curve describes the principle of Venetian composition, in a way comparable to the way music describes visual sensations."[12]

Goodnough's *Abduction* pictures shown at Tibor de Nagy Gallery in the early 1960s were relatively controversial while America's involvement in Vietnam, Cuba, and other hot spots inspired pictures bearing different titles. A canvas known simply as *Vietnam* reflects the chaos and confusion of America's war years in its bold power, in its angular, spear-like and battleax forms, in its shrapnel-like planes, in its vital energy, in its *lack* of unity, harmony, and balance, and in its explosive force, all of which evokes a mood of danger and peril. Reflecting the chaotic spirit of the times, Goodnough's picture reveals the awful potential of colliding slices of matter in a superheated space.

There were critics in those years who wondered if he would ever settle on one style, one mode of artistic endeavor. He was less concerned with that than he was in making pictures which showed his two-dimensional equations of kinetics and music. In 1966 he was awarded a $5000 grant of the National Council on the Arts. In the following year he was commissioned to execute a large canvas (9 x 32 feet) for the Manufacturers Hanover Trust Company in New York. His first solo show at the Whitney Museum took place in 1969, the year that he joined the faculty at Skowhegan Art School in Maine. Goodnough's list of credentials increased rapidly in the 1970s when abstraction was still reeling from the impact of Pop Art and new representational art styles. Although it was a time of great flux, Goodnough remained steadfast in his endeavor to create his special kind of abstract imagery. The year after his work was selected to represent this nation in the U.S. Pavilion at the Venice Bienale in Italy, he won a $3000 prize from The National Institute of Arts and Letters.

As the Vietnam War came to a halt and the raging inferno of violence began to simmer down, Goodnough's work became more ordered, more poetic, and even more luminous. Martin Bush states that for Goodnough "there are no rules, no limits—any color can be used if it works." Bush also points out that Goodnough's images are controlled through a highly developed sense of color and form because painting for him is self-discovery, and he arrives at an image through the art of painting itself."[13]

As Goodnough employed higher-key relationships in his shingles of color, that palette seemed to expand into other works consisting of larger and lighter spatial area, implying a less explosive, indeed, a quiet harmony. Many critics have referred to these works in terms of their airiness and the delicacy by which his relatively uniform notes of muted color seem to flicker and dance as they cluster loosely in columnar and ovoidal groups. Here orchestration is the salient quality of the picture. Goodnough's technique in producing these harmonious images is fascinating: working with a pencil, he draws in certain structural patch areas over a delicately rendered spatial ground. With the facet-like shapes arranged, he masks out their outer boundaries, then paints them in with acrylic pigment. The last sequence in working up his composition is painting select forms in oil. In this way the surface becomes a fascinating variety of textures and tilted planes. Whether Goodnough's image is powerfully rendered in strong chromatic contrasts and bold black lines or delicately manipulated crystals and slivers deftly orchestrated in luminous space, his procedure is relatively similar—each canvas

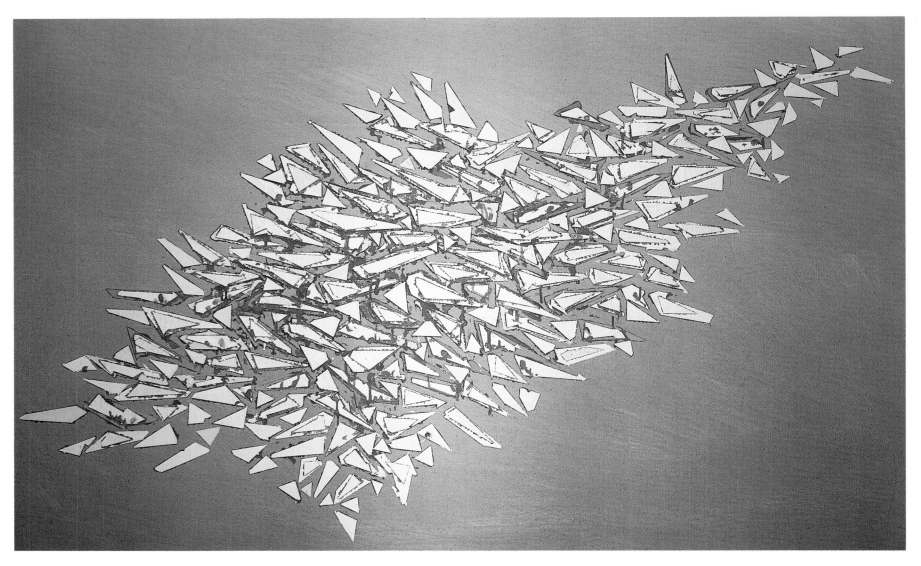

COLOR, WHITE, GRAY, 1981 acrylic and oil on canvas: 44 × 62 inches

UPLIFT, 1982 acrylic and oil on canvas: 46 × 62 inches

is unique.

In 1972 Goodnough's career was enhanced by a solo show at the André Emmerich Gallery in New York and by a John Simon Guggenheim Memorial Foundation Fellowship. A 100-foot mural in Cor-ten steel was created for Shawmut Bank in Boston in 1975, and a year later he was given a one-man show by Knoedler Contemporary. With praise pouring in from critics everywhere, Goodnough's pictures sold very well during this period. Many more solo shows followed; indeed, no less than 40 one-man shows took place during the decade of the seventies. At this time some of his most successful canvases entered the permanent collections of important museums in America and other countries. Today his work is found in the Art Institute of Chicago, the Corcoran Gallery of Art in Washington, the Metropolitan Museum of Art, and many more institutions, too numerous to mention here.

Martin Bush's monograph presents a man totally devoted to a lifelong task, that of making fine art. My own recent discussions with Goodnough have confirmed this continuous endeavor. Over the years the artist has moved from one studio to another, a situation which seems curious to some but not to Goodnough because he is always anxious to make something better—especially the art which, if not excellent, he destroys. He also rehabilitates his working environment if the need arises. When questioned about his frequent studio alteration or actual moves, he remarked appropriately that it was "probably a kind of restlessness." He went on to say that "moving to a new place gives me a new start, a change that would show up in my work."

Always looking for synthesis of ideas, a new start,

however motivated, Goodnough has kept his work from becoming old-fashioned, stagnant, or traditional. When the pages of *Art Forum* swelled with Greenberg's formalist doctrines, Goodnough's abstraction received top billing in the modernist art community. But as formalism gave way to structuralism, Post-structuralism, deconstructionism and the like, abstraction in general, even by a master like Goodnough, fell from the ranks of the avant-garde. Therefore, if abstraction has become a square peg in the round hole of Post-modernism, how do we view Robert Goodnough who created some of the best of it in America? It is probably best to disregard trends either pro or con and see Goodnough as a master the way Greenberg did before these recent years forced us to reconsider the term 'modern' in art. In this light we can use Hilton Kramer's words even fifteen years after he wrote them to describe Goodnough's contribution: "It has been fascinating over the years to watch this veteran abstract painter slowly and painstakingly dissolve the cubist substructure of his pictorial imagery in an effort to enlarge and release a more expressive two-dimensionality."[14] Indeed, that is the key to understanding Goodnough's work, the fact that he has always *released* the potential of two-dimensional pictorial surfaces. He makes pictures whose complex color shapes, spaces and lines pique our interest in a purely abstract visual realm. Some have said that his images seemed so overly intellectualized that they did not always communicate. Such limited perception was shallow since these pictorial explosions, symphonies and fugues fairly magnetize one's sensibilities in the way that Clive Bell professed that outstanding art should regardless of trends. Seldom does one view

Goodnough's canvases without heightened visual stimulation. In this way the viewer discovers the elusive aesthetic qualities extracted from Goodnough's secret art zone not exactly as Hilla Rebay searched for them but with new application for the spiritual principles of non-objective art.

So is it that in the 1980s the master continues as usual? Does he find a new stylistic twist? Not a blatant unprecedented manner turned opportunistically toward the rhetoric of Post-modernism but analysis does show compositional refinement, the results of which convey an even greater sense of harmonic balance and kinetic potential than before. Like Kenneth Noland and a few others whose continuing years of productivity have stimulated technical prowess rather than diminished it, Goodnough's inner sensibilities seem to have expanded over the years, resulting in artistic wisdom, the spontaneity of which transcends mere manipulative control. Perceptively captured at various moments, his images still consist of planes, color shapes, and lines, but there is now greater dimensional continuity as these pictorial elements interact. Realizing that these disparate components serve no function but for the sake of pure aesthetics, we the viewers become more sensitized to the role of arbitrary pictorial elements, perhaps a line which weaves magically in and out of spatial planes, large diffused shingles of color intersected and overlapped by smaller vibrating wedges, crystals and triangles, mass and form, broken, splintered, and fractured, but all seeming to emanate from an original core, an undefined universal life force originally thrust from unknown cohesive nuclei. And like the high-tech age in which we live,

these pictures seem, as their precedents did in the 1960s, to reflect the times, an era in which great unimaginable resources of energy are discovered and then manipulated by man with more complicated techniques each day. With ever increased experience, Goodnough controls ever greater resources, aesthetic substances as it were, from an unimaginable reservoir. The well known art critic Kenworth Moffett recently wrote of Goodnough's work: "He has been one of our very best painters since the 1950's."[15]

An outstanding example of Goodnough's work from the early 1980s is a canvas entitled *Landing*. The effect is a sense of internal force propelling large and small shingles of color into an ambiguous space. Here no uniform crystals gather in translatory motion. If at first glance we are confronted with an eruption of form and color, upon further examination we see that this complex design is truly elegant without reservation. The design is complex, yet controlled while color seeks an unrestricted dimension of its own and space is perceptually captured for a relative moment as it provides a synthetic two-dimensional forum for the reaction of Goodnough's elemental factors.

Goodnough's abstract dialectic has been resolved into a working structure for pictorial formats which are sometimes connective, sometimes disjunctive; but to be successful, they must probe beyond reality to evoke a sense of aesthetic movement, a quality which, as in musical scores, range from Brahms to Canonball Aderly. Goodnough's masterly treatment is captivating and, as in the case of any extraordinary criterion by which we judge the relative merit of other cultural productions, we make comparisons to other abstract media; thus, we

ABSTRACT MOVEMENT, 1983 acrylic and oil on canvas: 48 × 64 inches

perceive synthesis of the intangible for its own sake—
music for example. In Goodnough we perceive syn-
aesthetic images: juxtaposed shapes, color and line
with symphonies or jazz, wandering with anticipation
from one alluring polyphony to another. To understand
Goodnough's abstraction, we must sense movement,
implied and actual, human sensitivity to the improvisa-
tions of an artist whose creative images relate to the
visible and invisible universe. This spiritual process
provides a mental plateau for the contemplation of new
art each day. Conscious sensitivity to and knowledge of
these special qualities allows us to understand Greenberg when he said: "No matter what, he remains a
master-painter."[16] And we say, "Keep working, keep
moving, Mr. Goodnough, America needs you to keep
high art going."

FOOTNOTES

1. The Russian text *On the Spiritual in Art,* "O dukhovnom v iskusstve," was presented at the All-Russian Congress of Artists in St. Petersburg on 29 and 31 December, 1911 by Dr. Nikolai Kulbin on behalf of Kandinsky. Later it was published in the transactions of the Congress. The Städtische Galerie in Lenbachhaus in Munich preserves the original manuscript as part of the Kandinsky archives. The Russian text differs significantly from the well-known German edition, *Über das Geistige in der Kunst* printed by Piper in Munich in 1911 and again in 1912. From this printing came various translations including the English quoted here. For a contemporary source, see *The Life of Vasilii Kandinsky in Russian Art, A Study of* ON THE SPIRITUAL IN ART, edited by John E. Bowlt and Rose-Carol Washton Long and translated by John Bowlt, Oriental Research Partners, Newtonville, MA, 1984.

2. Kenneth C. Lindsay and Peter Vergo, eds., *Kandinsky: Complete Writings on Art* (Boston, MA: G. K. Hall & Co., 1982), pp. 145-146.

3. Joan M. Lukach, *Hilla Rebay, In Search of The Spirit in Art* (New York: George Braziller, 1983), p. 21.

4. Hilla Rebay, "The Beauty of Non-Objectivity," in *Modern Art and Modernism, A Critical Anthology,* edited by Francis Frascina and Charles Harrison (New York: Harper & Row, Publishers, 1982), p. 145; original source: *Solomon R. Guggenheim Collection of Non-Objective Paintings,* exhibition catalog, Philadelphia, PA: 1937), pp. 4-13.

5. For the most comprehensive study on the artist see Martin Bush, *Goodnough,* foreword by Clement Greenberg (New York: Abbeville Press, Publishers, 1982). This fine text serves as the basic source for biographical data used in this manuscript.

6. Clement Greenberg to Martin H. Bush, 19 January 1973, quoted from Bush, *Goodnough,* p. 12.

7. Lawrence Campbell, *Art News,* May 1955, p. 48.

8. Irving Sandler, *The New York School: The Painters and Sculptors of the Fifties* (New York: Harper & Row Publishers, 1978), p. 116.

9. John R. Lane, "Stuart Davis and the Issue of Content in New York School of Painting," *Arts,* February 1978, p. 156.

10. Ibid., p. 156.

11. Bush, p. 156.

12. Fairfield Porter, "Non-Objectivity and Realism," in *Fairfield Porter: Art in Its Own Terms, Selected Criticism 1935-1975,* edited by Rackstraw Downes (New York: Taplinger Publishing Co., 1979), pp. 92-93.

13. Bush, p. 121.

14. Hilton Kramer, *The New York Times,* 5 February 1972.

15. Moffett's Art Letter, July 1986.

16. Clement Greenberg, Foreword, in Martin Bush, *Goodnough,* p. 10.

LANDING, 1981-82 acrylic and oil on canvas: 82 × 216 inches

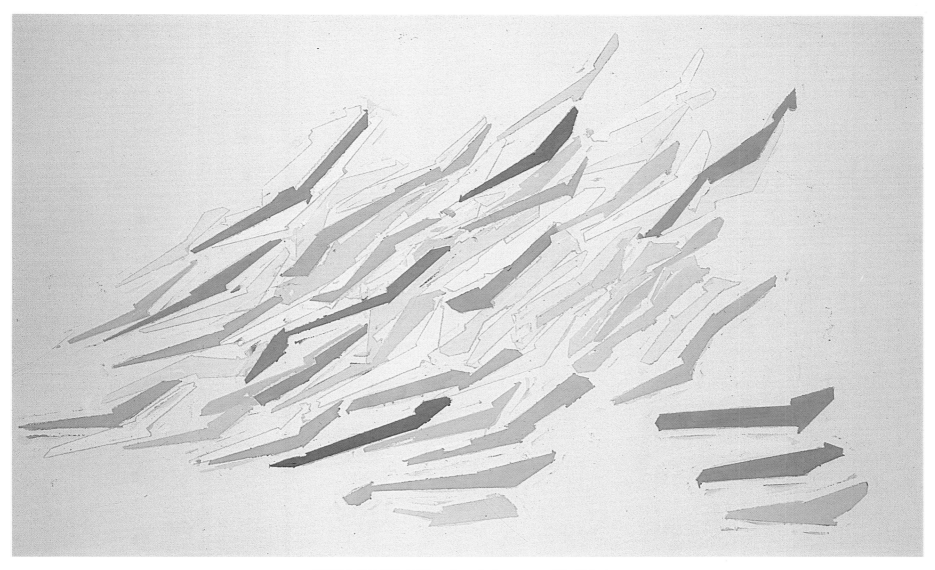

PASTEL SHAPES, 1985 acrylic and oil on canvas: 36 × 58 inches

EPILOGUE

Paintings can be illusionistic or non-illusionistic. They can suggest a third dimension or they can appear flat, as in design. I have worked both ways. Most of the great art of the past has been illusionistic. A horse painted on a canvas is obviously not a real horse, whereas a circle on a canvas is a circle—no third dimension need be involved as it is with the horse. At first I painted figurative pictures that depended partly on the third dimension for their existence. Then I painted abstract pictures in the sense that they depended on flatness rather than third dimension. Although some of the shapes on the canvas could be conceived of as floating in space, they actually suggest no thickness other than the thickness of the paint with which they are painted.

Recently I have been incorporating the third dimension—suggesting abstract but three-dimensional figures in space. These do not depend on the realistic aspect of figures, but on the spirit of what the figures might be involved in—energy, pathos, anger, affection, concern, and so forth. Sometimes I write words on these paintings, such as "war and peace," "break-through," etc. These expressions are intended to keep me enthused and more clear in my direction. When the painting is finished, the words may remain or be painted out. Some of the pictures that I am doing now combine shapes and colors used in earlier works with shapes from the middle period (smaller trapeziums), with an attempt to coordinate the two. Their message is perhaps more intense and heavy. They refer to paintings of the past, but I feel that they are more contemporary in direction. My recent sculptures are made with shapes similar to those in the paintings, and there is an interplay between the sculpture and the paintings. Painting, sculpture, and collage interact in my work.

—Robert Goodnough

SOLO EXHIBITIONS

1950 Wittenborn Gallery, New York, NY

1952 Tibor de Nagy Gallery, New York, NY

1953 Tibor de Nagy Gallery, New York, NY

1954 Tibor de Nagy Gallery, New York, NY

1955 Tibor de Nagy Gallery, New York, NY

1956 Art Museum, Rhode Island School of Design,
Providence, RI
Tibor de Nagy Gallery, New York, NY

1957 Tibor de Nagy Gallery, New York, NY

1958 Tibor de Nagy Gallery, New York, NY

1959 Dwan Gallery, Los Angeles, CA
Tibor de Nagy Gallery, New York, NY

1960 Art Institute of Chicago, Chicago, IL
Dwan Gallery, Los Angeles, CA
Ellison Gallery, Fort Worth, TX
Jefferson Place Gallery, Washington, DC
Tibor de Nagy Gallery, New York, NY

1961 Art Institute of Chicago, Chicago, IL
Dwan Gallery, Los Angeles, CA
The Nova Galleries, Boston, MA
Tibor de Nagy Gallery, New York, NY

1962 Dwan Gallery, Los Angeles, CA
Tibor de Nagy Gallery, New York, NY

1963 James Goodman Gallery, Buffalo, NY
Tibor de Nagy Gallery, New York, NY

1964 Art Gallery, University of Minnesota,
Minneapolis, MN
Art Gallery, University of Notre Dame, South
Bend, IN
Arts Club of Chicago, Chicago, IL
New Vision Centre Gallery, London, England
Tibor de Nagy Gallery, New York, NY
USIS Gallery, American Embassy, London,
England

1965 Tibor de Nagy Gallery, New York, NY

1966 Gertrude Kasle Gallery, Detroit, MI
Tibor de Nagy Gallery, New York, NY

1967 Art Gallery, University of Notre Dame, South
Bend, IN
Reed College, Portland, OR
Tibor de Nagy Gallery, New York, NY

1968 Tibor de Nagy Gallery, New York, NY

1969 Albright-Knox Art Gallery, Buffalo, NY
Axiom Gallery, London, England
Cayuga Museum of History and Art, Auburn,
NY
Galeria Colibri, San Juan, Puerto Rico
Galerie Simonne Stern, New Orleans, LA
Gertrude Kasle Gallery, Detroit, MI
Tibor de Nagy Gallery, New York, NY
Whitney Museum of American Art, New York,
NY

1970 Galerie Simonne Stern, New Orleans, LA

RZY, 1986 acrylic and oil on canvas: 48 × 78 inches

6H4, 1986 acrylic and oil on canvas: 34 × 62 inches

J. Kasmin Limited, London, England
Tibor de Nagy Gallery, New York, NY

1972 Andre Emmerich Gallery, New York, NY
Gertrude Kasle Gallery, Detroit MI
Harcus Krakow Gallery, Boston, MA
Nicholas Wilder Gallery, Los Angeles, CA
Syracuse University Lubin House Gallery, New York, NY

1973 Andre Emmerich Gallery, New York, NY
Gallerie Ulysses, Vienna, Austria

1974 Andre Emmerich Gallery, New York, NY
David Mirvish Gallery, Toronto, Canada
Everson Museum of Art, Syracuse, NY
Gertrude Kasle Gallery, Detroit, MI
Harcus Krakow Gallery, Boston, MA
Tibor de Nagy Gallery, Houston, TX

1975 Andre Emmerich Gallery, New York, NY
David Mirvish Gallery, Toronto, Canada
Galerie Andre Emmerich, Zurich, Switzerland
Harcus Krakow Rosen Sonnabend Gallery, Boston, MA
Ulysses Gallery, Vienna, Austria
Watson/de Nagy Gallery, Houston, TX

1976 Douglas Drake Gallery, Kansas City, MO
Harcus Krakow Gallery, Boston, MA.
Knoedler Contemporary Art, New York, NY
Waddington Galleries II, London, England
Watson/de Nagy Gallery, Houston, TX
William Sawyer Gallery, San Francisco, CA

1977 David Mirvish Gallery, Toronto, Canada
M. Knoedler & Company, New York, NY
Watson/de Nagy & Company, Houston, TX

1978 Douglas Drake Gallery, Kansas City, MO
Edwin A. Ulrich Museum of Art, Wichita State University, KS
Fontana Gallery, Narberth, PA
Harcus Krakow Gallery, Boston, MA
Hokin Gallery, Chicago, IL
Lee Hoffman Gallery, Birmingham, MI
Nina Freudenheim Gallery, Buffalo, NY

1979 Hokin Gallery, Chicago, IL
Hokin Gallery, Palm Beah, FL
Klondaridis Inc., Toronto, Canada
Watson/de Nagy & Company, Houston, TX

1980 André Emmerich Gallery, New York, NY

1982 André Emmerich Gallery, New York, NY

1983 Klonaridis Gallery, Toronto, Canada

1984 The Watson Gallery, Houston, TX

1985 Klonaridis Gallery, Toronto, Canada
Tibor de Nagy Gallery, New York, NY
Galerie Elca, London, Montreal, Quebec

1986 Klonaridis Gallery, Toronto, Canada
Galerie Elca, London, Montreal, Canada
The Watson Gallery, Houston, TX
Tibor de Nagy Gallery, New York, NY

1987 The Gallery at Lincoln Center, New York, NY
R. H. Love Modern, Chicago, IL

PUBLIC COLLECTIONS

Albright-Knox Art Gallery, Buffalo, NY
The Aldrich Museum of Contemporary Art, Ridgefield, CT
Andrew Dickson White Museum of Art, Cornell University, Ithaca, NY
Art Institute of Chicago, Chicago, IL
Art Gallery, University of Notre Dame, South Bend, IN
Baltimore Museum of Art, Baltimore, MD
Birmingham Museum of Art, Birmingham, AL
Cayuga Museum of History and Art, Auburn, NY
The Chase Manhattan Bank, New York, NY
Ciba-Geigy Chemical Corporation, Ardsley, NY
Corcoran Gallery of Art, Washington, DC
Edwin A. Ulrich Museum of Art, Wichita State University, Wichita, KS
Everson Museum of Art of Syracuse and Onondaga County, Syracuse, NY
Griffith Art Center, St. Lawrence University, Canton, NY
Herbert F. Johnson Museum of Art, Cornell University, Ithaca, NY
Hirshhorn Museum and Sculpture Garden, Washington, DC
J. B. Speed Art Museum, Louisville, KY
Kresge Art Center Gallery, Michigan State University, East Lansing, MI
Manufacturers Hanover Trust, New York, NY
Memorial Art Gallery of the University of Rochester, Rochester, NY
The Metropolitan Museum of Art, New York, NY
Museum of Art, Pennsylvania State University, University Park, PA

Museum of Art, Rhode Island School of Design, Providence, RI
Museum of Fine Arts, Boston, MA
Museum of Fine Arts, Houston, TX
Museum of Twentieth Century Art, Vienna, Austria
The Museum of Modern Art, New York, NY
National Museum of American Art, Washington, DC
Newark Museum, Newark, NJ
New York University Art Collection, New York, NY
North Carolina Museum of Art, Raleigh, NC
Owens-Corning Fiberglas Corporation, Toledo, OH
Portland Museum of Art, Portland, ME
Purdue University, Lafayette, IN
Rose Art Museum, Brandeis University, Waltham, MA
S. C. Johnson Collection of Contemporary American Art, Racine, WI
The Solomon R. Guggenheim Museum, New York, NY
State University of New York, Cortland, NY
Syracuse University Art Gallery, Syracuse, NY
University Art Museum, University of California, Berkeley, CA
University Gallery, University of Minnesota, Minneapolis, MN
Virginia Museum of Fine Arts, Richmond, VA
Wadsworth Atheneum, Hartford, CT
Weatherspoon Art Gallery, University of North Carolina, Greensboro, NC
Whitney Museum of American Art, New York, NY
Wichita Art Museum, Wichita, KS

BIBLIOGRAPHY

EXHIBITION CATALOGS AND BROCHURES

Bush, Martin H. *Goodnough*. Houston: Watson/de Nagy & Company, 1978.

_____. *Robert Goodnough*. New York: Andre Emmerich Gallery, 1980.

Bush, Martin H. and Moffett, Kenworth. *Goodnough*. Wichita: Ulrich Museum of Art, Wichita State University, 1973.

"Business Buys American Art." New York: Whitney Museum of American Art, 1960.

Collages by American Artists. Muncie, Indiana: Art Gallery, Ball State University, 1971.

Enders, Gaetana. *Eighteen Contemporary Masters*. Ottawa, Canada: United States Embassy, 1977.

Friedman, B.H. *Goodnough*. Los Angeles, CA: Dwan Gallery, 1960.

Goodnough. Houston, TX: Watson/de Nagy & Company, 1979.

Goodnough: An Exhibition of Recent Paintings and Sculpture. Montreal, Quebec: Galerie Elca London, 1986.

Goodnough: An Exhibition of Recent Paintings and Sculpture. Toronto, Ontario: Klonaridis, Inc. 1986.

Goodnough, Major Works: 1957-1968. New York: Tibor de Nagy Gallery, 1985.

Goodnough: Recent Work. Houston, Texas: The Watson Gallery, 1986.

Goodnough Sculpture. New York: The Gallery at Lincoln Center, 1986.

Goodnough Sculpture. New York: Tibor de Nagy Gallery, 1986.

Highlights of the 1969-70 Art Season. Ridgefield, CT: The Aldrich Museum of Contemporary Art, 1970.

Koslow, F.A. and W. Harding. *Henry David Thoreau as a Source of Artistic Inspiration*. Lincoln, MA: De Cordova and Dana Museum, 1984.

Lauck, Anthony. *Looking Backward from Robert Goodnough*. South Bend, IN: University of Notre Dame, 1967.

Meyers, John Bernard. *One Two Three: (An Homage to Pablo Casals), Twelve Serigraphs by Robert Goodnough*. San Juan, Puerto Rico: Galeria Colibri, 1969.

Moffett, Kenworth. *Abstract Painting in the 70's: A Selection*. Boston, MA: Museum of Fine Arts, 1972.

Robert Goodnough. Detroit, MI: Gertrude Kasle Gallery, 1972.

Robert Goodnough. London: Axiom Gallery, 1969.

Robert Goodnough. New York: Andre Emmerich Gallery, 1972.

Robert Goodnough. New York: Syracuse University Lubin House Gallery, 1972.

Robert Goodnough. Zurich, Switzerland: Galerie Andre Emmerich, 1975.

Robert Goodnough: Recent Paintings. Detroit, MI: Gertrude Kasle Gallery, 1972.

Seitz, William C. *The Art of Assemblage*. New York: The Museum of Modern Art, 1961.

Steinberg, Leo. *The New York School: Second Generation*. New York: The Jewish Museum, 1957.

Williams, Ben F. *American Paintings Since 1900 from the Permanent Collection*. Raleigh, NC: North Carolina Museum of Art. 1967.

ARTICLES AND STATEMENTS
by Robert Goodnough

"About Painting." *Art and Literature: An International Review*. (Autumn 1965): 119-127.

"The Artist." *Robert Goodnough: Recent Paintings*. Exhibition catalog. New York: Syracuse University Lubin House Gallery, 1972.

"Baizermand Makes a Sculpture." *Art News*. (March 1952): 40-43.

Bush, Martin. "Talking with Robert Goodnough" in *Goodnough*. New York: Abbeville Press, 1982: 161-240.

"David Hare Makes a Sculpture." *Art News*. (March 1956): 46-49.

"Franz Kline Paints a Picture." *Art News*. (December 1952): 36-39.

"Herbert Ferber Makes a Sculpture." *Art News*. (November 1952): 40-43.

"Jackson Pollock Paints a Picture." *Art News*. (May 1951): 38-41.

J7, 1986 acrylic and oil on canvas: 74 × 118 inches

"Reviews and Previews: Seymour Lipton." *Art News*. (October 1950).

"Robert Goodnough Art in New York and Chicago." *Antiques and the Arts Weekly*. (13 February 1987): 32.

"Statement." *It Is*. (Spring 1958): 19.

"Two Postscripts." *Artforum*. (September 1965): 32.

Weller, Allen S. in "Goodnough." *Art USA Now*, Lucerne, Switzerland: C.J. Bucher, Ltd., 1962: 11, 317.

Wilson, Stuart. "Goodnough is critical of modern life." *The Montreal Downtowner*. (17 December 1986): 22.

ARTICLES AND REVIEWS

Adrian, Dennis. "New York: Robert Goodnough." *Artforum*. (May 1966): 50.

Art International. (April 1964): 56.

"Artist Gives Work to Museum: Show Remains to May 12." *Citizen Advertiser*, Auburn. (May 1969).

"As He Pleases." *Newsweek*. (19 March 1962): 116.

Ashton, Dore. "Art." *Arts & Architecture*. (March 1960): 35.

_____. "Art." *Arts & Architecture*. (May 1962): 7.

_____. "Art: Paintings by Robert Goodnough." *The New York Times*. (6 January 1959).

_____. "Recent Exhibition at the Tibor de Nagy Gallery." *Arts & Architecture*. (March 1961): 6.

_____. "Robert Goodnough." *Art Digest*. (15 November 1952): 23.

_____. "Robert Goodnough." *Studio International*. (1 July 1962): 8.

_____. "Robert Goodnough at the Tibor de Nagy Gallery." *Studio International*. (June 1968): 322.

Bates, Catherine. "Getting Up to Date." *The Montreal Star Entertainments*. (10 November 1973).

Battcock, Gregory. "Robert Goodnough." *Arts Magazine*. (May 1968): 67.

Bell, Jane. "Robert Goodnough." *Arts Review*. (January 1975).

Benedikt, Michael. "Robert Goodnough." *Art News*. (March 1965): 12.

"The Best of the Best." *Time*. (6 July 1962): 48-49.

Blakeston, Oswell, "Robert Goodnough." *The Arts Review*. (8 November 1969): 23.

Borden, Lizzi. "Robert Goodnough." *Artforum*. (April 1972): 85.

Bourdon, David. "What's Goodnough Celebrating?" *The Village Voice*. (8 March 1976).

Brach, Paul. "Robert Goodnough." *Art Digest* (1 February 1952): 18.

Brumer, Miriam. "Robert Goodnough." *Arts Magazine*. (May 1969): 65.

_____. "Goodnough at Tibor de Nagy." *Arts Magazine*. (March 1970): 62.

Burton, Scott. "Robert Goodnough." *Arts News*. (March 1966): 14

_____. "Robert Goodnough." *Art News*. (Summer 1968): 15.

Bush, Martin H. "An Interview with Robert Goodnough." *Arts Magazine*. (February 1979): 136-141.

_____. "Goodnough." *Art International*. (March 1974): 32-35, 53-54.

_____. "Robert Goodnough's Collages." *Arts Magazine*. (April 1982).

Butler, Barbara. "Brach, Goldberg, Goodnough, Mitchell." *Arts Magazine*. (June 1956): 48-49.

Butler, Susan. "Goodnough Paintings Intelligent, Sophisticated." *Houston Chronicle*. (26 April 1974).

Campbell, Lawrence. "Robert Goodnough." *Art News*. (May 1955): 48.

_____. "Robert Goodnough." *Art News*. (1 April 1970): 21.

Conrad, Barnaby III. "Robert Goodnough." *Art World*. (February 1977): 6.

Crossley, Mimi. "Review Art." *The Houston Post*. (11 March 1977).

_____. "Walk in Painting." *The Houston Post*. (September 1976).

Curtis, Charlotte. "Artists Visit Their Friends at Chase Manhattan." *The New York Times*. (18 April 1969).

De Montebello, Philippe. "Two Contemporary Paintings." *The Museum of Fine Arts, Houston: Bulletin*. (June 1970): 47-48.

Devree, Howard. "To Help Artists." *New York Times*. (14 June 1959).

Driver, Morley. "Robert Goodnough, a Name Predicted for Greatness." *The Detroit News*. (6 March 1966).

Drysdale, Susan. "Abstract 'artmaking' in the '70's." *The

Christian Science Monitor. (24 April 1972): 9-10.

"Eleven Paintings, Collage by Goodnough, To Go On Display January 18 at Reed." *Portland Oregonian.* (15 January 1967).

"Exhibit of Goodnough Paintings at Everson." *The Moravia Republican-Register.* (January 1975).

Faulkner, Joseph W. "Goodnough's Spirited Art Stirs Up Thoughts of the New York School." *Chicago Tribune.* (15 March 1964).

Findlater, Richard. "Visions of Serenity, Carefully Crafted." *Detroit Free Press.* (13 January 1974).

Forge, Andrew. "Know-how." *New Statesman.* (28 August 1964): 294.

"Fourth National Mini Bank Opens." *Wichita Eagle Beacon.* (15 July 1974).

Frachman, Noel. "Robert Goodnough." *Arts Magazine.* (April 1977).

Fried, Alexander. "Art on the Dark and Bright Sides." *San Francisco Examiner.* (April 1976).

"Galerie André Emmerich." *Neue Zürcher Zeitung,* Zurich, Switzerland. (11 January 1975).

Genauer, Emily. *New York Post.* (28 February 1976).

"Gifts From New Yorkers Add to WSU's Collection." *Wichita Eagle Beacon.* (12 November 1978).

Glueck, Grace. "Into the Mainstream, Everybody." *New York Times.* (15 June 1969).

_____. "Kootz is Closing Art Gallery: Will Write About His Career." *New York Times.* (8 April 1966).

_____. "Names of Artists in Biennale Released." *New York Times.* (9 July 1970).

_____. "Previews." *Art in America.* (January 1972): 41.

_____. "Reviews." *Art in America.* (January-February 1972): 37-41.

_____. "Venice—Off With the Show." *New York Times.* (4 October 1970).

Goldin, Amy. "Robert Goodnough." *Arts Magazine.* (May 1966): 65.

"Goodnough Exhibit." *The Times—Picayune,* New Orleans. (19 January 1969).

Gollin, Jane. "Robert Goodnough." *Art News.* (Summer 1969): 14.

Gordon, Alastair. "The New Vision Centre." *The Connoisseur.* (September 1964): 50.

Gray, Cleve. "New Venture—The Hilton Hotel Collection." *Art in America.* (April 1963): 124.

Guest, Barbara. "Blue Stairs: Poem." *Art in America.* (October 1956): 47-48.

Hakanson, Joy. "Goodnough and Yunkers." *The Detroit News.* (13 March 1966).

_____. "The Art World." *The Detroit News.* (23 November 1969).

_____. "Robert Goodnough." *Detroit Free Press.* (13 January 1974).

Harithas, James. "Notes on Goodnough's New Paintings." *Art Spectrum.* (February 1975): 24.

Hartranft, Ann. "Goodnough Has Top Show at Everson." *Syracuse Herald Journal.* (12 January 1975).

Hess, Thomas B. "United States Paintings: Some Recent Directions." *Art News Annual.* (1956): 17.

"Hochmodern und Archaisch Alt." *Badener Tagblatt.* (4 February 1975).

Hughes, Robert. "Abstract Energy." *Observer.* London. (23 August 1964).

Judd, Donald. "Robert Goodnough." *Arts Magazine.* (February 1961): 53.

_____. "Robert Goodnough." *Arts Magazine.* (May 1962): 98.

Kachur, Lewis. "Robert Goodnough Paintings in Waddington II." *Arts Review.* (4 March 1975).

Kind, Joshua. "One-Man Shows in Chicago." *Art News.* (May 1964): 21.

Klinger, Betty. "Artist Goodnough." *The Citizen.* (4 July 1976).

Kramer, Hilton. "The Return of 'Handmade' Painting." *New York Times.* (April 1972).

_____. "Robert Goodnough." *New York Times.* (28 March 1970).

_____. "Robert Goodnough." *New York Times.* (5 February 1972).

_____. "Robert Goodnough." *New York Times.* (6 March 1976).

LaFarge, Henry A. "Robert Goodnough." *Art News.* (November 1950): 47.

Langser, Jules. "Everts, Jawlensky, Goodnough." *Art News.* (Summer 1960): 56.

Marshal, W. Neil. "Robert Goodnough: More Than Easel Painting." *Arts Magazine.* (September 1975).

Mayer, Ralph. "Robert Goodnough." *Art Digest.* (15 March 1954): 19.

McDonald, Robert. "Robert Goodnough's Paintings." *San Francisco Examiner.* (9 October 1976).

Moffett, Kenworth. "Notes on Goodnough's Recent Work." *Art International.* (20 October 1970): 54-56.

Morris, George N. "Nova Gallery Stages Goodnough Exhibit." *Worcester Daily Telegram.* (17 April 1961).

Moser, Charlotte. "Variations on Goodnough's Theme are Refreshingly Open, Direct." *Houston Chronicle.* (30 November 1975).

_____. "Glow of Authority." *Houston Chronicle.* (21 January 1979).

Muck, Gordon. "Art Views and News." *Syracuse Post-Standard.* (23 December 1974).

Munsterberg, Hugo. "Robert Goodnough." *Arts Magazine.* (January 1960): 49.

Myers, John Bernard. "The Perils of Hindsight." *Art Forum.* (October 1980): 29-31.

_____. "What Is a Subject?" *Art Journal.* (Spring 1977): 41

O'Doherty, Brian. "O! Say Can You See." *Newsweek.* (11 January 1965): 78.

O'Hara, Frank. "Goodnough Gazed on Euclid Bare." *Art News.* (March 1954): 18, 64.

"Painted—Poetry at Everson." *Citizen Advertiser.* Auburn, New York. (January 1975).

Pease, Roland F., Jr. "Robert Goodnough." *Metro 9.* (April 1962): 57-61.

Perry, Art. "Abstractions a Mixed Bag." *The Province.* Toronto, Canada. (16 September 1975).

Porter, Fairfield. "Robert Goodnough." *Art News.* (February 1952): 42.

_____. "Robert Goodnough." *Art News.* (November 1952): 45.

_____. "Robert Goodnough." *Art News.* (January 1959): 10.

Preston, Stuart. "Contemporary Cross-Currents." *New York Times.* (15 January 1961).

Purdie, James. "The Sixties' Rebels are Building Anew." *The Globe and Mail.* Toronto, Canada. (18 October 1975).

Raynor, Vivien. "Robert Goodnough." *Arts Magazine.* (May 1963): 107-108.

_____. "Robert Goodnough." *Arts Magazine.* (March 1964): 67.

_____. "Robert Goodnough." *Arts Magazine.* (May-June 1965): 56-57.

"Reizvolle Kontraste." *Schweiz Handles-Zeitung,* Zurich, Switzerland. (February 1975).

"Robert Goodnough." *Magazine of Art.* (October 1952): 258-259.

"Robert Goodnough." *New York Times.* (October 1974).

"Robert Goodnough." *New York Times.* (2 November 1924).

"Robert Goodnough Art in New York and Chicago." *Antiques and the Arts Weekly.* (13 February 1987): 32.

"Robert Goodnough Exhibit." *The Times—Picayune,* New Orleans (8 November 1970).

Rose, Barbara. "Abstract Painting Now, 'Refiners!'" *Vogue.* (July 1970): 34.

_____. "The Second Generation: Academy and Breakthrough." *Artforum.* (September 1965): 53-63.

Rosenberg, Harold. "The American Action Painters." *Art News.* (December 1952): 22-23, 48-50.

_____. "The Art World." *The New Yorker.* (26 August 1967): 90.

Rosenblum, Robert. *Arts Magazine.* (February 1956): 53.

Russell, John. "London Art." *The Sunday Times.* London. (23 August 1964).

Sandler, Irving H. "Robert Goodnough." *Art News.* (January 1960): 12.

_____. "Robert Goodnough." *Art News.* (January 1961): 11.

_____. "Robert Goodnough." *Art News.* (April 1963): 12.

Sawin, Martica. "Robert Goodnough." *Art Digest.* (15 May 1955): 29.

Schuyler, James. "Is There an American Print Revival? New York. *Art News.* (January 1962): 36-37.

_____. "Robert Goodnough." *Art News.* (January 1956): 51.

Steinberg, Leo. "Contemporary Group of New York Painters at Stable Gallery." *Arts Magazine.* (January 1956). 46-48.

12H, 1986 painted aluminum: 18 × 38 inches

Swenson, G.R. "Robert Goodnough." *Art News*. (March 1962): 12.

_____. "Robert Goodnough." *Art News*. (February 1964): 8.

Tyler, Parker. "Robert Goodnough." *Art News*. (March 1957): 8.

_____. "Is Today's Artist With or Against the Past?" *Art News*. (June 1958): 42.

"University Gallery Seeks Contributions for Purchase of Painting Count Down." *St. Paul Dispatch*. (22 February 1967).

Wasserman, Emily. "New York: Robert Goodnough." *Artforum*. (May 1970): 78-79.

_____. "Robert Goodnough." *Artforum*. (Summer 1968): 55-56.

Westfall, S. "Art Reviews." *Arts Magazine*. (October 1982).

Wilson, Stuart. "Goodnough is critical of modern life." *The Montreal Downtowner*. (17 December 1986): 22.

Young, Vernon. "Robert Goodnough." *Arts Magazine*. (May 1957): 51.

"Zürcher Galerienspiegel." *Basler Nachrichten*. (29 January 1975).

"Zurich." *Artequia*. (April 1975).

BOOKS AND REFERENCE WORKS

Alloway, Lawrence. *Network: Art and the Complex Present*. Ann Arbor, MI: UMI Research Press, 1984.

Baur, John I.H. *Nature in Abstraction*. New York: The MacMillan Company, for the Whitney Museum of American Art, 1958.

Blesh, Rudi. *Modern Art, USA: Man—Rebellion—Conquest 1900-1956*. New York: Alfred A. Knopf, 1956.

Bowlt, John E. and Rose-Carol Washtonhong, ed. *The Life of Vasili Kandinsky in Russian Art A Study on the Spiritual in Art*. Translated by John Bowlt, Oriental Research Partners: Newtonville, Massachusetts, 1984.

Bush, Martin H. *Goodnough*. New York: Abbeville Press, 1982.

Cummings, Paul. *Dictionary of Contemporary American Artists*. New York: Alfred A. Knopf, 1956.

Downes, Rackstraw, ed. *Fairfield Porter: Art in Its Own Terms, Selected Criticism 1935-1975*. New York: Taplinger Publishing Co., 1979.

Emanuel, Muriel, et al, eds. *Contemporary Artists*. New York: St. Martin's Press, 1983.

Goodrich, Lloyd and John I. H. Baur. *American Art of Our Century*. New York: Whitney Museum of American Art, 1961.

_____. *American Art of the 20th Century*. London: Thames and Hudson, 1962.

Guest, Barbara. "Robert Goodnough" in Friedman, B.H., ed. *School of New York: Some Younger Artists*. New York: Grove Press and Evergreen Books, 1959.

Guest, Barbara and B. H. Friedman. *Goodnough*. Paris: Editions Georges (Fall 1962).

Harrison, Helen A. *Larry Rivers*. New York: Harper & Row, 1984.

Janis, Harriet, and Rudi Blesh. Collage: *Personalities—Concepts—Techniques*. Philadelphia, PA: Chilton Company, 1962.

Kramer, Hilton. *The Revenge of the Philistines, Art and Culture, 1972-1984*. New York: The Free Press, A Division of Macmillan, Inc., 1985.

Krantz, Les, ed. American Artists: *An Illustrated Survey of Leading Contemporary Americans*. New York: The Krantz Company Publishers, Inc., 1985.

Kultermann, Udo. *The New Painting*. New York: Frederick A. Praeger, 1969.

Lindsay, Kenneth C. and Peter Vergo, eds. *Kandinsky: Complete Writings on Art,* Boston, MA: G.K. Hall & Co., 1982.

Lippard, Lucy R. *Ad Reinhardt*. New York: Harry N. Abrams, 1981.

Lukach, Joan M. *Hilla Rebay, In Search of the Spirit of Art*. New York: George Braziller, 1983.

Rose, Barbara. *American Painting: The 20th Century*. Lausanne, Switzerland: Skira, 1969.

Sandler, Irving. *The New York School: The Painters and Sculptors of the Fifties*. New York: Harper & Row, 1978.

_____. *The Triumph of American Painting: A History of Abstract Expressionism*. New York: Praeger Publishers, 1970.

Seuphor, Michel. *Dictionary of Abstract Painting: With a History of Abstract Painting*. New York: Paris Book Center, 1957.

Shipley, James R., and Allen S. Weller. *Contemporary American Painting and Sculpture 1969*. Urbana, IL: University of Illinois Press, 1969.